IT'S A GIRL

AN OWNER'S MANUAL
FOR YOUR NEW BABY

BY MARTIN BAXENDALE

TODAY'S BEAUTY TIP
IS YOGHURT AND
BANANA FACE-MASK...

IT'S A GIRL! AN OWNER'S MANUAL
FOR YOUR NEW BABY:
© Copyright 2005 Martin Baxendale.
Published by Silent But Deadly Publications,
21 Bisley Road, Stroud, Glos. GL5 1HF,
England.

ISBN 0 9539303 9 4

Printed in England by Stoate & Bishop Printers Ltd,
The Runnings, Cheltenham, Glos. GL51 9NH.

CONTENTS

FOREWORD

With care and regular servicing, your NEW BABY is
guaranteed to provide many years of trouble-free
operation and countless hours of family fun and
entertainment.*

Indeed, once you come to appreciate the many
labour-saving and money saving advantages of
owning a NEW BABY, you'll wonder how you ever
managed without one!

No more valuable hours wasted in front of the TV
or sleeping whole nights away! No more time and
money wasted on dressing up for nights on the
town! No more wasted time and effort spent driving
or walking to the pub, to parties, or to other
tedious social events! No more much-needed cash
wasted on pints and gin-and-tonics, on over-priced
cinema tickets, expensive restaurant bills, new
cars, or time-wasting holidays in the sun!

*NOTE: This guarantee of 'trouble-free operation'
is of course a load of absolute cobblers. It in
no way affects your statutory right to whinge,
whine, grumble, develop bags under your eyes,
become unreasonably argumentative and snappy, or
(in extreme circumstances) to wrap up your
belongings in a spotted hankie and run away from
home.

DELIVERY NOTE: We apologise for any delay in delivery of your NEW BABY but regret that we can accept no liability for circumstances beyond the manufacturer's control; such as chronic under-funding and under-staffing of the Health Service, shortage of maternity beds, unavailability of hospital anaesthetists, etc. All complaints regarding delivery should be directed to your nearest available politician and/or your local Health Authority.

GETTING STARTED: If you've never owned a NEW BABY before, don't panic! Anyone can master the basic operating instructions in a matter of days, and soon you'll be changing nappies and preparing midnight feed bottles as though you'd been doing it all your life. Indeed, after a week or two it'll feel like you *have* been doing it all your life. Good luck with your NEW BABY, and God help you.

UNPACKING AND ASSEMBLING YOUR NEW BABY

We recommend that you unpack your NEW BABY in the presence of a manufacturer-approved technician (qualified midwife/doctor) as this can prove a fiddly job and you may need an extra pair of hands.

1: Carefully remove protective wrapping (see opposite page)

2: Disconnect NEW BABY (A) from midwife/doctor (B)

3: Connect power supply unit (C) or (D) to power input port (E)

4. Attach overflow/disposal unit (F) to outlet valves (G), ensuring accurate location and secure fixing to prevent leaks

5. Connect NEW BABY to parental partner (H), to waiting grandparents (I) and to any other visiting relatives (J)

6: Locate earplugs (K) firmly in your ears (L) and do not remove for at least first 12 months

7: Disconnect all money from bank account and insert into cash tills of Mothercare, Boots the Chemist, Early Learning Centre, etc.

8: Wave goodbye to social life, uninterrupted sleep, dreams of buying flashy new car, etc

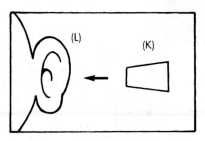

UNPACKING NOTE: Take care when removing the protective packaging from your NEW BABY. *Do not discard,* as it may come in handy later.

WARNING! WIRING AND POWER SUPPLY: Please note that your NEW BABY does *not* come complete with batteries or mains lead. *Under no circumstances* attempt to connect your NEW BABY to a mains supply or try to run the unit on either rechargeable or non-rechargeable batteries. Your NEW BABY is *not* designed to operate on these types of power source, and any unauthorised electrical connection or installation may invalidate the lifetime warranty.

9

BASIC FEATURES

Take time to familiarize yourself with the basic features of your NEW BABY. A thorough working knowledge of these features is essential before moving on to the more advanced operating modes and functions.

NOTE: According to individual model, your NEW BABY may be equipped with Dad's/Mum's type nose, Dad's/Mum's type ears, Dad's/Mum's type eyes, etc, depending on current availability of manufacturing components. This in no way affects operating or servicing procedures as these parts are fully compatible and interchangeable.

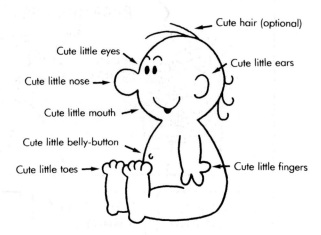

Cute hair (optional)

Cute little eyes

Cute little ears

Cute little nose

Cute little mouth

Cute little belly-button

Cute little toes

Cute little fingers

Loading point

Fuel tank

Unloading point

Once you've mastered the basic features, here are a few simple *Fun Things for Beginners* that you can try out with your NEW BABY: CUDDLING; KISSING; TICKLING; FEEDING; CHANGING; STAYING AWAKE ALL NIGHT; WATCHING BANK BALANCE GO INTO THE RED.

HERE! BURP THE BABY FOR ME!

BURP THE BABY?

FULL TUMMY

JUST PUT THE BABY OVER YOUR SHOULDER...

...AND PAT THE BABY ON THE BACK!

THAT'S IT! THANKS!

BURP!!

WELL THAT WAS EASY! I DON'T KNOW WHY YOU DIDN'T DO IT YOURSELF.

11

CAUTION! Your NEW BABY incorporates many useful and entertaining features, but you should be aware of its operational limitations. Most importantly, your NEW BABY, although the latest state-of-the-art technology, is *not* equipped to play compact discs, receive or record telephone messages (either at home or in-car), receive satellite television transmissions, hold loose leaf Filo-fax pages, microwave, or defrost frozen food

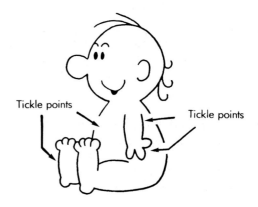

Tickle points

Tickle points

Kissing points

Kissing points

PORTABILITY: Your NEW BABY is a *fully portable lap-size* model. Unfortunately, the basic model does not come complete with carrying handles. However, these are available as an optional accessory, as are various add-on wheel options for increased portability (see page 28).

WARNING! Do not attempt to use ears (see diagram on opposite page) as carrying handles — this applies *only* to *rabbits*. Repeatedly picking up and carrying your NEW BABY by the ears may result in excessive wear on these components, possible criminal prosecution and/or headlines in the national Press.

12

ADVANCED FEATURES

In addition to the many exciting basic features offered by your NEW BABY, you'll find that a wide range of more technically advanced 'special' functions have also been incorporated for your convenience and enjoyment.

'BAG-FULL' SIGNAL: Operation of this signal indicates that the overflow/disposal unit is full and requires replacement with a fresh unit. **Warning!** Continued running with a 'full bag' will result in noisy and inefficient operation.

AIR-FRESHENER FUNCTION: Your NEW BABY is equipped with a fully automatic long-life air-freshener function. Simply place NEW BABY in house or apartment and stale cooking smells, lingering odours of tobacco smoke, dirty ashtrays, and domestic pets will be covered up and banished by the parenthood-fresh scents of wet nappies, spilt milk, baby powder, etc.

WAIL!

Automatic 'Bag-full' signal

Automatic Air-freshener function

13

EARLY- MORNING/MIDDLE-OF-THE-NIGHT ALARM FUNCTION: This is another fully automatic built-in feature of your NEW BABY. *Note:* The alarm *cannot* be re-set or cancelled.

Snooze-mode button: A standard alarm clock-radio feature which allows an extra few minutes' lie-in by delaying alarm-repeat; unfortunately, *not* available as a standard feature on your NEW BABY.

WAIL!

AUDIO SYSTEM: We regret that your NEW BABY is *not* equipped to play audio cassettes, standard-play or long-play records, or compact discs, in mono, stereo or quadrophonic reproduction. Neither can your NEW BABY pick up AM or FM radio transmissions without considerable modification.
However, your NEW BABY *will* play 'Teddy Bears Picnic', 'Pop Goes the Weasel' and many more state-of-the-art clockwork recordings if connected to an optional cord-pull operated audio unit.

IN-CAR ENTERTAINMENT: Your NEW BABY is easily adaptable from a home-based or portable unit to an *in-car entertainment* system. Simply attach securely to rear passenger seat using any of the widely available 'baby car seat' fixing kits; then sit back and sample the pleasures of hi-fidelity screaming and wailing as you drive.

15

RUNNING GAMES ON YOUR MICRO-BABY

Your NEW BABY is not just a useful appliance. Although basically an 'expensive business' machine, your NEW BABY will also run some exciting and exhilerating games for hours of family fun and enjoyment.

These are just some of the many popular games programs which will run on your NEW BABY (minimum RAM memory required, 64K):

"TICKLE-TICKLE"
"PEEK-A-BOO"
"BOUNCY-BOUNCY"
"UPS-A-DAISY"
"COOCHY-COO"

Fast-moving audio-visual games of quick reflexes and reponses. Select single-player mode, or compete with your partner for highest smile-and-chuckle score!

Note: Unfortunately these games programs are not yet available on floppy disc, cassette or ROM cartridge, so must be programmed by hand.

BEEP!

BEEP!

16

STORAGE WHEN NOT IN USE

When not in use, we recommend that you store your NEW BABY in a warm, dry place and protect with a dust-cover to prevent unsightly accumulations of dead flies, dust, etc., and to maintain optimum operating temperature. Specially designed storage units ('cot' type and 'pram' type) are available at extra cost (see 'Add-on accessories', page 28).

WARNING! Despite its compact size, your NEW BABY is *not* designed to store away *beneath kitchen worksurfaces.*

X WRONG

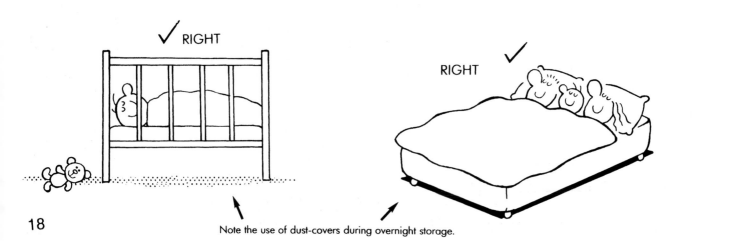

✓ RIGHT

RIGHT ✓

Note the use of dust-covers during overnight storage.

19

PLUMBING-IN YOUR NEW BABY

Although your NEW BABY is designed to be fully portable, permanent plumbing-in for ease of operation is theoretically possible. Do, however, bear in mind that the advantages of permanent installation will be offset by the disadvantages of reduced operational flexibility. See also, Warning below.

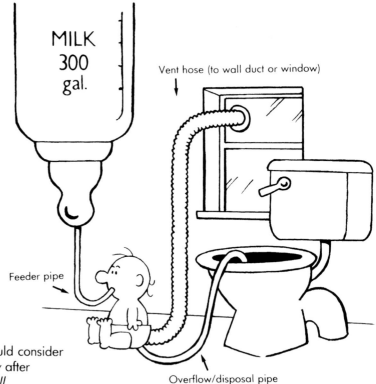

MILK 300 gal.

Vent hose (to wall duct or window)

Feeder pipe

Overflow/disposal pipe

WARNING! We strongly advise that you should consider permanently plumbing-in your NEW BABY *only* after seeking professional advice, preferably from *all* of the following: Qualified plumber; doctor or mid-wife; health visitor; social worker; Chief Constable; local magistrate; Crown Court judge; nearest branch of the NSPCC.

PROGRAM SELECTION

Your NEW BABY has *two* basic operating programs: *'Sleeping'* and *'Awake'*. Take care to select the appropriate program to suit the particular function or operating mode required from your NEW BABY (see also, 'A guide to operating modes', page 16).

PROGRAM	HOW TO SELECT
'Sleeping' Most popular program for putting feet up, watching TV, getting babysitter in, going out, going to bed, etc.	Select 'Sleeping' program as follows: Bath your NEW BABY, wrap warmly, feed, wind, cuddle, rock in arms, put down in cot, sing lullaby; pick up again, change nappy, wind, cuddle, rock, put in cot; change partners; sing lullaby, pick up, feed, wind, change nappy, put down; pick up, wind, put down, sing; sigh with relief, tiptoe out of room, cross fingers, touch wood
'Awake' A less popular program, but essential for most everyday modes of operation	Any of the following procedures will initiate 'Awake' program: Loud noises (e.g. doorbell or 'phone ringing, door closing, cat purring, pin dropping, breath being held); sitting down in front of TV; sighing with relief; pouring drinks; telling babysitter "We'll only be an hour or so"; crawling into bed; closing eyes; falling asleep

A GUIDE TO OPERATING MODES

Once the 'Awake' program has been selected (see previous page), your NEW BABY is ready to switch into a wide range of useful and entertaining operating modes.

BASIC MODES: You should learn to recognise and cope with these more basic operational features within the first few weeks:
GURGLING MODE ☆ SMILING MODE ☆ CHUCKLING MODE ☆ CRYING MODE ☆ WHINGING MODE ☆ FEEDING MODE ☆ BURPING MODE ☆ PUKING MODE ☆ POOHING MODE ☆ WEEING MODE ☆ RUNNY NOSE MODE
Important Note: 'Poohing' and 'Weeing' modes are fully automatic and may operate during 'Sleeping' program *as well as* during 'Awake' program.

ADVANCED MODES: These more complicated advanced operating modes should *only* be attempted by NEW BABY owners with at least several months experience of operation at basic mode levels:
SITTING-UP AND FALLING-OVER MODE ☆ CRAWLING MODE ☆ STANDING-UP AND FALLING-OVER MODE ☆ WALKING AND FALLING-OVER MODE ☆ BICYCLE-RIDING MODE ☆ SPEECH MODE ☆ GOING-OUT-TO-WORK-AND-BRINGING-SOME-MONEY-INTO-THE-HOUSE MODE

Recommended operating positions

———— 'Sleeping' program ————

———— 'Awake' program ————

———— Servicing and cleaning ————

(see pages 22-26)

PROBLEMS IN OPERATION

LEAKS: Due to basic design faults, your NEW BABY is unfortunately prone to leakage problems. As excessive build-up of humidity may seriously damage the luxury exterior-finish of your NEW BABY, take care to change the de-humidifier/overflow/waste disposal unit at regular intervals. **Warning!** Under no circumstances should you try to prevent leaks or drips by fitting new washers.

NOISY OPERATION: Noisy operation is *perfectly normal*. However, in the event of excessive noise developing during operation, we advise fitting an approved *silencer unit* type (A) or type (B) (see diagram). This is a straightforward installation which may be tackled in the home without expert help or specialised tools.

TEETHING PROBLEMS: We regret that your NEW BABY will eventually develop teeth. Sorry! See 'Noisy operation'.

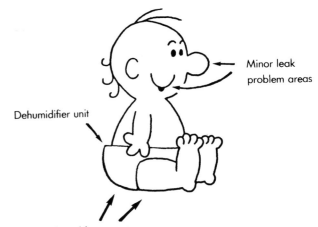

Minor leak problem areas

Dehumidifier unit

Major leak problem areas

(A)

(B)

Fitting your NEW BABY with silencer unit type (A) 'Dummy' or type (B) 'Teething comforter'

25

INTERFERENCE: Your NEW BABY is manufactured to strict electrical industry standards which should ensure that it will not interfere with TV or radio reception when in operation. However, we *cannot* guarantee that your NEW BABY will not interfere with your *social life, normal sleep patterns* and *financial situation*.

Note: In the event of severe or prolonged interference with your sleep, due to noisy operation, try moving your NEW BABY further away from your sleeping area, as in diagram (A). Alternatively, you may find that moving your NEW BABY *closer* to your sleeping area, as in diagram (B), may have virtually the same effect.

(A)

(B)

FAULT DIAGNOSIS CHART

SYMPTOM	POSSIBLE CAUSE	RECOMMENDED ACTION
Crying	Hunger	Feed your NEW BABY
Crying	Wind	Burp your NEW BABY
Crying	Damp	Change overflow/waste disposal unit
Crying	Smelly	Change overflow/waste disposal unit
Crying	Tired	Select 'Sleep' program (see page 15)
Crying	Teething	Refer to page 18, 'Teething problems'
Not crying	Probably asleep	Sigh with relief, put up feet in front of TV, pour large drink, crawl into bed

SAFETY IN OPERATION

VENTILATION: Always ensure adequate ventilation of rooms where your NEW BABY is in operation, to prevent hazardous build-up of noxious fumes; *especially* when changing the overflow/waste disposal unit following operation of 'Poohing' mode. Anyone overcome by fumes while working in close proximity to a NEW BABY should immediately be removed from the source of the hazard, using breathing apparatus if necessary; revive with oxygen and large brandies. In severe cases (e.g. where an inexperience male operative is overcome by fumes while changing the overflow/disposal unit) hospitalization and psychiatric counselling may be required to help overcome the trauma.

EXPLOSION HAZARD! During changing of overflow/waste disposal unit following 'Poohing' mode, beware of *fire* and *explosion* hazards due to abnormally high build-up of fumes. *Avoid naked flames* and *do not smoke* during nappy-emptying!

WARNING! Do not leave your NEW BABY unsupervised for prolonged periods while in the various operating modes, particularly in advanced modes such as 'crawling' and 'walking', as this may result in severe damage both to the NEW BABY unit itself and to surrounding furnishings, fragile valuables, small domestic pets, etc.

PROTECTIVE GEAR: For your personal safety, we strongly advise the use of industrial protective clothing, face masks, breathing apparatus, etc. during the more hazardous and messy operations such as changing the overflow/waste disposal unit, spoon-feeding, burping, and dealing with leaky nose problems. Avoid wearing new, expensive or difficult-to-clean clothes *at all times.*
Use of ear-plugs is also advisable during at least the first 12 months of operating your NEW BABY, and these are likely to soon become compulsory under new EEC health-and-safety regulations.

NOTE: For additional peace of mind, we recommend covering all carpets, soft furnishings, car seats, etc. with protective splash-sheets (heavy-duty polythene, waxed canvas, or nuclear industry-standard lead sheeting is advisable). Alternatively, put all furniture, carpets, valuables, etc. into storage until your NEW BABY is at least 21 years old; or purchase a blow-torch and steam-hose for removing stubborn stains and encrusted food residues.

ROUTINE SERVICING

Regular servicing is vital for continued trouble-free operation of your NEW BABY. Fortunately, most routine servicing may be carried out by the owner in the home with the aid of a standard NEW BABY tool kit (when unpacking your NEW BABY, *please note* that NEW BABIES do *not* come complete with tool kit; so don't go rummaging around in the packaging looking for one).

RECOMMENDED TOOL KIT:

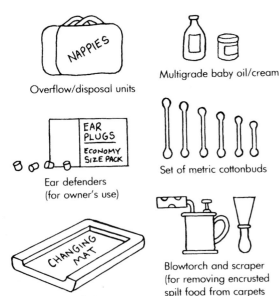

Overflow/disposal units

Multigrade baby oil/cream

Babysitters

Inspection lamp

Ear defenders (for owner's use)

Set of metric cottonbuds

Set of metric filler units

Static-free wipes

Inspection/servicing ramp

Blowtorch and scraper (for removing encrusted spilt food from carpets and furnishings)

Silencer unit

Healthy bank balance

Booze (optional; for lubrication of NEW BABY owners, to ensure continued trouble-free operation of owners)

MAIN LUBRICATION POINTS

(A) Wet, dribbly bits
(B) Pongy bits
(C) Wrinkly bits
(D) Red, rashy bits
(E) Any bits which develop
    annoying squeaks
    during operation

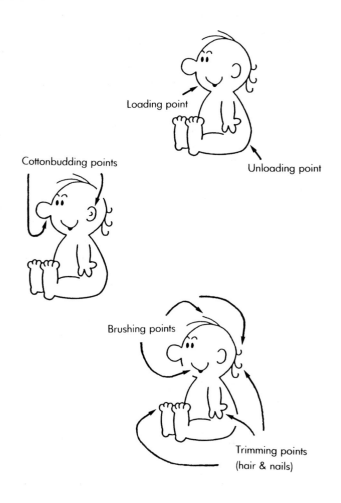

Loading point

Unloading point

Cottonbudding points

Brushing points

Trimming points
(hair & nails)

34

BATHTIME IS SO BORING!

YAWN!

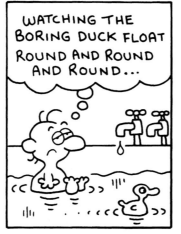

WATCHING THE BORING DUCK FLOAT ROUND AND ROUND AND ROUND...

STUPID BORING DUCK!

SPLASH!

THE BABY'S FOUND OUT ABOUT SPLASHING!

35

D.I.Y. SERVICING PLAN:

Every 5 minutes

● Check that all Kissing points (see page 9) have been kissed at least once since last 5-minute service.

● Check NEW BABY's finger-clutching function by stroking palm of BABY's hand with finger.

● Check operation of NEW BABY's Smiling and Chuckling modes using tickle controls (page 9).

Every 1 – 2 hours

● Check condition of overflow/disposal unit and renew as necessary.

● Check other potential leak problem areas (see page 17) at the same time.

Every 2 – 4 hours

● Check fuel level and top-up as necessary; avoid over-filling, which may cause problems when your NEW BABY switches to Burp mode.

Every 24 hours

● Clean down all external surfaces and visible working parts (see 'Washing instructions', page 26). Don't forget cottonbudding points (page 23).

● Oil or grease all lubrication points (page 23).

● Check and adjust alignment of hair (in the event of a temporary lack of hair, wax and polish head).

Every 2 – 4 weeks

● Check for appearance of first teeth (see 'Teething problems', page 18).

● Check length of fingernails and toenails; trim as necessary.

● Check condition of bank balance; lubricate self with large drinks to ensure continued smooth running of NEW BABY owner.

CHECKING LEVELS IN OVERFLOW/DISPOSAL UNIT

It is *absolutely essential* that the levels in the overflow/disposal unit are checked at frequent intervals and the unit replaced as necessary *without delay.*

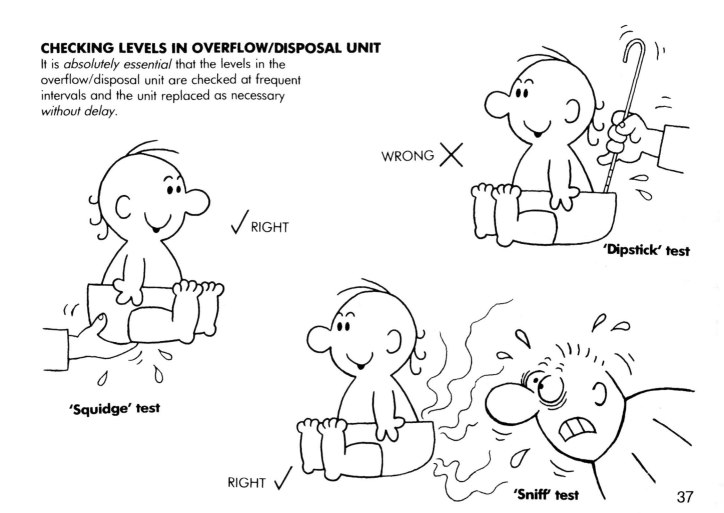

✓ RIGHT

'Squidge' test

WRONG ✗

'Dipstick' test

RIGHT ✓

'Sniff' test

37

WASHING INSTRUCTIONS

 Hand-wash only (low temperature)

 Do not machine-wash

 Do not dry-clean

 Do not spin-dry

 Do not tumble-dry

 Dry flat (do not hang out to dry)

 Do not iron

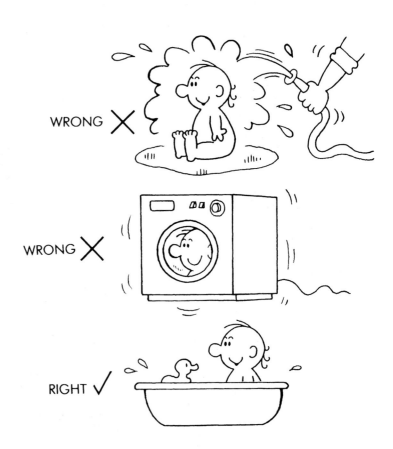

WRONG ✗

WRONG ✗

RIGHT ✓

LOOK! AT LAST I CAN GET BACK INTO MY POSH DRESSES...

...INSTEAD OF HAVING TO SLOP AROUND IN BAGGY PREGNANCY-WEAR ALL THE TIME!

BLEUGH!!

REPLACEMENT SPARE PARTS

Always ensure that you use *approved* replacement spare parts when servicing your NEW BABY. Use of unauthorised replacement units may cause problems in operation and/or attract disapproving looks from health visitors.

Do not try to cut costs with non-standard cheap replacement servicing units.

41

OPTIONAL ADD-ON ACCESSORIES

A wide range of add-on accessories are available
to enhance and extend your NEW BABY's performance.
In all cases, fitting these optional units is a
simple procedure well within the scope of any
competent D.I.Y. enthusiast.

Baby work station

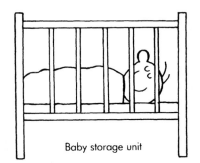
Baby storage unit

Portable baby storage unit

Auto-fixing kit (turns
your NEW BABY into an
in-car entertainment system)

Add-on wheels for
increased portability

Carrying handles

Audio unit

EXTENSION SPEAKERS:

Your NEW BABY may be fitted with 'Baby alarm' type *extension speakers* to enhance your enjoyment of your NEW BABY's unique sounds-system capabilities. Imagine the convenience of being able to channel hi-fidelity sound reproduction into every room in the house! Imagine your visitors' surprise and pleasure as, using a built-in tape-deck facility, you instantly play-back the most exciting bits of your NEW BABY's repertoire for their enjoyment and appreciation!

'Walkman' baby alarm with mobile extension speakers

Baby alarm

SNORE!
SNORE!

SNORE!
SNORE!

Extension speakers

45

SECURITY IDENTIFICATION CODE

As a basic security precaution (in case you should
mislay your NEW BABY or confuse it with similar
units in a crowd) we strongly advise that you
allocate a personal security identification code
to it. Examples: "Janet", "John", etc. (Note: we do
not recommend using your post code for this purpose).

Since stencilling, engraving or invisible security-
pen-marking your NEW BABY with its personal
identification code is not advisable, enter your
choice of code here as a permanent record for
future reference.

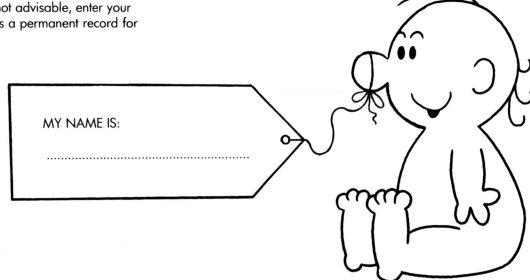

MY NAME IS:

....

TECHNICAL SPECIFICATIONS

Maximum speeds
Crawling mode: ½ mph
Baby-walker mode: 1 mph
Toddling mode: 1½ mph

Average fuel consumption
6 fl oz – 24 fl oz per day,
according to age of Baby

Capacities
Fuel tank: 2 fl oz – 10 fl oz,
according to age of Baby
Overflow/disposal unit: Av. 1 fl oz

Recommended lubricants
Multigrade baby oil/baby cream

Audio output
Gurgling mode: 3 watts (4 decibels)
Chuckling mode: 5 watts (7 decibels)
Crying mode: 60 watts (300 decibels)

ARTIFICIAL ADDITIVES
Your NEW BABY contains no artificial additives
(artificial preservatives, flavourings, etc). We
recommend that you keep it that way.